Extreme Weather

FLOODS

Martha London

DiscoverRoo
An Imprint of Pop!
opbooksonline.com

abdobooks.com

Published by Pop!, a division of ABDO, PO Box 398166, Minneapolis, Minnesota 55439. Copyright © 2020 by POP, LLC. International copyrights reserved in all countries. No part of this book may be reproduced in any form without written permission from the publisher. Pop!™ is a trademark and logo of POP, LLC.

Printed in the United States of America, North Mankato, Minnesota.

052019
092019

THIS BOOK CONTAINS RECYCLED MATERIALS

Cover Photo: iStockphoto
Interior Photos: iStockphoto, 1, 5, 6, 8–9, 10 (top); 10–11 (wave), 11 (bottom), 13, 15, 22, 23, 24, 25, 28, 29 (house), 29 (checkmarks), 29 (car), 29 (wave), 29 (wallet and key), 29 (television), 29 (bottom), 30, 31; Mirco Vacca/Alamy, 7; Bob Galbraith/AP Photo, 10 (bottom); Shutterstock Images, 11 (top), 14, 16–17, 20, 27; Darryl Dyck/The Canadian Press/AP Images, 19; Xinhua/Alamy, 21

Editor: Connor Stratton
Series Designer: Sophie Geister-Jones
Library of Congress Control Number: 2018965057
Publisher's Cataloging-in-Publication Data

Names: London, Martha, author.
Title: Floods / by Martha London.
Description: Minneapolis, Minnesota : Pop!, 2020 | Series: Extreme weather | Includes online resources and index.
Identifiers: ISBN 9781532163937 (lib. bdg.) | ISBN 9781532165375 (ebook)
Subjects: LCSH: Floods--Juvenile literature. | Flood control--Juvenile literature. | Natural disasters--Juvenile literature.
Classification: DDC 551.489--dc23

WELCOME TO DiscoverRoo!

Pop open this book and you'll find QR codes loaded with information, so you can learn even more!

Scan this code* and others like it while you read, or visit the website below to make this book pop!

popbooksonline.com/floods

*Scanning QR codes requires a web-enabled smart device with a QR code reader app and a camera.

TABLE OF CONTENTS

CHAPTER 1
HOW FLOODS FORM

A flood is when a large amount of water flows onto land that is normally dry. Most of the time, extra water soaks into the ground. Or it runs off into a body of water, such as a river. But sometimes there is more water than those areas can hold. A flood happens.

A flood can cover a whole neighborhood with water.

WATCH A VIDEO HERE!

Rain that falls at a rate of 1 inch per hour can be enough to start a flood.

Many events can cause floods. Floods can happen anywhere rain falls. Melted snow can make rivers overflow. A dam can break and let water rush out. Large storms on the coast cause floods too.

DID YOU KNOW?

Even a beaver dam can cause a river to flood!

Water floods out of a broken dam.

Sometimes floods happen without warning. These types of floods are called flash floods. Heavy rain can cause

Vehicles can get caught on the road during a flash flood.

a flash flood. Flash floods form within 6 hours of rain starting. Floodwater can climb up to 30 feet high.

CAUSES OF FLOODS

Heavy rainfall is a common cause of floods. But floods can happen for many different reasons.

HEAVY RAINFALL

BROKEN DAM

MELTING SNOW

STORM SURGE

CHAPTER 2
WHERE FLOODS FORM

Most floods happen near rivers or

coasts. Areas near rivers are called

floodplains. These low areas get many

floods. But they can also prevent floods

from spreading. Both floodplains and

LEARN MORE HERE!

wetlands act as sponges. They hold large amounts of water. They stop the water from reaching other areas.

Flat land near rivers is more likely to flood.

Some cities are built on floodplains.

Floods are more common in cities.

Cities have a lot of pavement. Unlike

soil, pavement cannot soak up water.

When rain falls on pavement, it can't

soak into the ground. Instead, the water

DID YOU KNOW?

A new kind of pavement helps stop flooding. Water can flow through it into the ground.

In 2017, a hurricane caused flooding in Houston, Texas.

spreads and covers more land. Cities on floodplains have even more risk. The flat land makes it easy for water to spread.

Floods happen all around the

world. But they are more common in

certain areas. Bangladesh is a country

People try to travel through floodwaters in Bangladesh.

in southern Asia. This country faces the greatest risk of flooding. It has seasons of huge rains. It also has many rivers.

CHAPTER 3
EFFECTS

Floodwater can travel as fast as 10 miles per hour. At that speed, floods can carry away trees and cars. Floods can pull dirt from under a building. When that happens, the building can fall apart.

LEARN MORE HERE!

Some floods have the power to uproot trees.

DID YOU KNOW?

It takes only 6 inches of moving water to sweep people off their feet.

Mold grows on a chair after a flood.

Floods damage the insides of buildings as well. When water enters homes, mold can grow. Mold can eat away furniture and parts of a house. It can also make people sick.

Floodwater spreads disease. It often carries germs. They can get into drinking water and cause illnesses.

In 2017, rains in western Africa caused a mudslide.

Some flooding is helpful. Rivers have lots of silt and dirt. The silt and dirt are filled with nutrients. When rivers flood, these nutrients flow onto the land. Nutrients make the land better for growing plants.

Rice is one crop that grows well in flooded land.

When the Nile River floods, it helps plants along its banks grow.

DID YOU KNOW?

In ancient Egypt, the Nile River flooded every year. The silt from the flood made farming possible in the desert.

However, scientists worry that floods are getting worse. Earth's average temperature is rising. Warmer temperatures can cause stronger storms. These storms can lead to worse floods.

In addition, climate change can cause

Not all floods are helpful for crops. Heavy floods can make it hard for farmers to grow food.

A glacier melts in Argentina.

glaciers to melt. More water enters the

ocean. The rising sea levels can cause

floods along the coast.

CHAPTER 4
STAYING SAFE

Floods can be dangerous. It is important to be prepared. Weather stations warn people about floods. If the water gets high enough, people may need to leave the area.

COMPLETE AN ACTIVITY HERE!

A woman evacuates a flood in Southeast Asia.

People build walls out of sandbags to help stop flooding.

Sometimes flash floods happen in minutes. There might not be time to evacuate. So, people try to find a safe place nearby. They move to higher ground. People also avoid driving through the flood. If people prepare, they can help keep themselves safe during a flood.

Flood Safety Checklist

 Evacuate if necessary.

 Stay away from moving water.

 Keep important things safe and dry.

 Listen to the news for weather updates.

FLOOD AHEAD

MAKING CONNECTIONS

TEXT-TO-SELF

Is the area where you live likely to flood?
Why or why not?

TEXT-TO-TEXT

Have you read books about other kinds
of natural disasters? What do they have in
common with floods? How are they different?

TEXT-TO-WORLD

Not all floods are harmful. What is one
example of a place where flooding could
be good?

GLOSSARY

climate change – differences in Earth's weather patterns, often including a rising temperature.

floodplain – a flat area near a river that floods often.

nutrient – matter that humans, animals, and plants need to stay strong and healthy.

pavement – a human-made covering over the ground, such as a sidewalk.

silt – sandy soil carried by rivers.

wetland – an area often covered with water.

INDEX

ONLINE RESOURCES

popbooksonline.com

Scan this code* and others like it while you read, or visit the website below to make this book pop!

popbooksonline.com/floods

*Scanning QR codes requires a web-enabled smart device with a QR code reader app and a camera.